CW01523796

Come Undone

A Steamy Age-Gap Romance

Nichole Rose

Nichole Rose

Kindle Edition

Copyright © 2022 by Nichole Rose

All rights reserved. This book or any portion thereof may not be reproduced or used in any manner whatsoever without the express written permission of the author except for the use of brief quotations in a book review.

All characters appearing in this work are fictitious. Any resemblance to real persons, living or dead, is purely coincidental.

Cover by Yoly at Cormer Covers

Contents

About the Book

Love is just a 1-900 number away for this curvy girl and the man of her dreams...

Arwen Grayson

Two weeks ago, I met the man of my dreams.

By day, he's my crazy hot roofer.

By night, he's the wicked man who drives me wild over the phone.

The only problem?

I have no idea if he's the same man or not.

And I'm running out of time to find out.

Today, I plan to learn the truth once and for all.

Even if I have to play dirty to do it.

Granger Vaughn

Two weeks ago, I met the curvy girl of my dreams.

But she doesn't know that the man she greets with a sweet smile every morning is the same one who drives her wild on the phone at night.

I got myself into this mess.

It's time to get myself out of it.

I just hope like hell she doesn't kick me out of her life when I confess.

Because I can tolerate a lot...but I won't survive losing her.

She's meant to be mine.

Come Undone is a quick and dirty short romance featuring a not-so-secret identity and an intimate relationship that burns hot and fast between a curvy girl and the older man of her dreams. It is a standalone addition to the *Love Bites* series.

Chapter One

Granger

"Hey, baby. It's Arwen."

I grip the phone tightly in my hand as Arwen Grayson's sweet voice whispers down the line. Desire stirs, hitting me like a fist at the breathless hitch in her voice. Every pleasantry I promised I'd exchange with her tonight leaves my mind in an instant. The only thing left behind is burning hunger and the need to hear her come undone for me one more time.

"I need you naked." My voice strains with the need to make her come. Tension knots my shoulders, the ache for release cinching my balls up tight. Even the skin across my back feels stretched too tight.

"Tex." The nickname I gave her the first time I called sounds like little more than an erotic sigh tumbling from her lips. "I hoped you would call again."

I bite back a groan at the thought of her naked and waiting in her bed for me, her nipples hard, her dark curls spread across the pillow, her big blue eyes dark with desire, her thick thighs like porcelain against the dark blue counterpane. Goddamn. I want to see that sight for myself.

Good luck with that, asshole, I think.

A girl like Arwen isn't going to give a motherfucker like me the time of day. To her, I'm just a lonely pervert at the other end of the line. Nothing could be further from the truth, of course. She doesn't know it, but I'm the same man she's greeted with a smile at her front door every day for the last two weeks.

I'm her roofer. And a complete jackass.

I was captivated the moment I saw her. But like an asshole, I didn't approach her. Instead, I eavesdropped as she chatted with her roommates about her new job as a phone sex operator. She was nervous and didn't know what to expect. She's a virgin, but she needs the cash. As soon as I heard that, my protective instincts went into overdrive.

I know what kind of filthy shit men want from women, especially innocent little lambs like Arwen. They're not getting it from her, not even on the phone. It's been years since I was last with anyone, but I spent half the afternoon trying to find the company she said she worked for, and then I did what needed to be done.

It's a damn good thing I own a successful business because I'm her only client.

I tell myself I only call to protect her, but I'm a liar.

That very first night, I convinced her to tell me her fantasies instead of acting out mine. She opened up to me in a way I never expected, allowing me a glimpse into her secret sexual desires. I've been hooked on her since. No, that's not true. I'm head over heels in love with this girl. She's as curious as she is sweet, as sexy as she is adorable.

Two weeks later, I'm no closer to telling her who I really am than I was that first night.

The way I see it, I'll be lucky if all she does is stick her stiletto up my ass when she finds out I not only eavesdropped on her private conversation but then acted on what I overheard. No, there won't be any getting out of this mess, and she definitely won't be letting me carry her to bed to make love to her like I truly desire once she finds out how badly I've abused her trust.

Sad fact is...all I'll ever have of her is this: a once-a-night phone call.

If this is all I can have of her, I'll take it, though, consequences be damned.

"Are you wet for me, Arwen?" I pop the button of my jeans and jerk them down, freeing my cock. I want to be a gentleman and make this about her, but who am I kidding? I am no gentleman, and my cock is already throbbing for release. I wrap my hand around my length and pump, hissing as pleasure shoots through me hard and fast.

Arwen's response comes as little more than a needy whimper in my ear. "Yes, Tex."

"That's real good, sweetheart." I love how easily she responds to me and how much she opens up to me on these calls. She trusts me with her body, even if only over the phone. What I make her feel, what I make her do, isn't just a call to her. *I'm* not just a call to her. I see the truth in her eyes every morning and in the subtle smile that never entirely leaves her face. I fucking love knowing I put that smile there.

Watching it fade when she realizes I'm the one she's been talking to isn't appealing to me. And yet I can't seem to stop calling her either. I don't want her talking to anyone who isn't me.

"How do you want me tonight, Tex?" she asks.

A thousand different possibilities run through my mind in an erotic parade. I want her above me, riding my cock hard. I want her on her knees in front of me, screaming as I fuck her from behind. I want her writhing in pleasure beneath me, begging me not to stop.

"On your knees," I growl, fisting my cock.

A rustling comes down the line as she complies with my demand. I can't help but grin at the confirmation that she wants this just as much as I do. I think most phone sex operators lie their way through every encounter. They fake it until it's over and then move on to the next. Arwen hasn't faked a damn thing with me since the beginning.

"I love the way you look in the center of that big bed," I murmur into the telephone, stroking my cock slowly. "You're a seductress with your head thrown back and your perfect little breasts on display. My cock aches for you already."

Her breath hitches.

"You like knowing that, don't you?" I ask.

"Yes."

I grin at her honest answer. "Touch yourself for me, Arwen. Slide your hand down that curvy little body and feel how wet you already are for me."

She moans softly as she touches herself.

I close my eyes, imagining her hand and perfectly manicured pink nails trailing down her curvy body before disappearing between her legs.

"Tex. I'm so wet," she groans.

"Good." My balls ache at the surprise in her tone, as if she can't quite believe she really responds to me this way. As if she can't believe just the anticipation of my call made her so hot.

I ensured that response the first night I called, coaxing her into confessing her deepest desires and then using every trick I knew to talk her into back-to-back orgasms. If she has to do this to get herself through grad school while feeling like she's carved out a little independence, I want it to be a good memory for her.

"I want you to fuck yourself with your fingers," I order her. "Ride your hand like it's mine. Can you do that for me, darlin'?"

"Oh, God," she groans, her breath rate increasing audibly. "Yes, Tex."

"Then do it, little one. Pretend your hand is mine and finger yourself for me." I wait until she moans again, letting me know that she's doing exactly as I demanded. As soon as I hear that sweet sound, I pump my cock, desire burning through me even hotter than before. "Your pretty little pussy is so tight around my fingers. I can feel your walls clenching every time I press deeper."

She moans wordlessly in response.

"Your juices are trickling down my hand already, darlin'. The entire room smells like sex, like you. I'm starving for you, Arwen," I rasp, closing my eyes and letting the truth of that statement wind its way through me. "I see the way your head rolls on your shoulders, exposing that lovely throat to me every time I press against your g-spot. I want to sink my teeth into your neck and mark you there. You want it too, don't you?"

"Please." Her confirmation is nothing more than a deep groan.

"Come for me, darlin', and maybe I will," I tease her, my voice thick with the desire to do precisely that. The thought of her skin beneath my lips, of pressing my tongue to the pulse in her throat, of seeing my mark on her...Jesus.

"I'll leave proof on that beautiful body that you're mine, little one. Mine to touch. Mine to please. Mine to *fuck*."

"Oh!" She cries out in surprise at the emphasis I put on that word.

I expected nothing less. I may be a jackass, but I know her. I know what she wants, what she craves, what turns her on, and what makes her tick. She wants to be possessed and cherished at the same time. She wants to be claimed and adored, loved beyond all reason. She's fiercely independent, but she's shy and sweet too. She needs someone to steady her and help her fly, someone willing to let her explore every facet of herself inside the bedroom and out.

I'm dying to be that man for her. Fuck, if she let me, I'd never tell her no or hold her back. I'd teach her everything she wanted to learn and then some. No one would hurt her. No one would frighten her.

"After you come on my fingers for me, I'm going to bury my head between your legs and eat you until you can't take any more. Let me have it, little one," I command, my hand flying over my cock now. "Let me taste that sweet pussy again."

"Oh, oh, Tex!" she cries out.

I fist my cock, listening in satisfaction as she comes for me.

I don't let myself go over with her, though.

I haven't earned that right. Not yet.

Chapter Two

Arwen

"He called again last night," I announce, bounding into the kitchen. Bright light filters into the room from the large bay windows, lighting little dust motes hovering in mid-air.

My two roommates and best friends turn to look at me, matching expectant expressions on their faces. I don't immediately give them the details they want, though. Instead, I amble toward the coffee pot on the slate-gray counter and pour a cup before bringing it to my nose and inhaling.

Tex called again.

I'm a twenty-three-year-old woman, but I fight the urge to squeal like a high school girl with her first crush. Every night for the last two weeks, he's called. And every night, he's given me multiple mind-blowing orgasms. From phone sex.

I didn't even know that was possible until him.

I'm a virgin. Thanks to my dad and my brothers, not to mention my uncles and cousins, the likelihood of me dying a virgin is high. Taking a job as a voice model—or phone sex operator—is not something I would typically do. But graduate school is expensive, and I don't want to depend on my parents forever. I want to make my own money and be my own person. So I took the job until my part-time on-campus position reopens this fall.

Tex has been my only caller so far. And he calls me every night. From the very first call, he's been all about me and what I want. How I want to be touched, what I fantasize about. His sexy Southern twang is almost hypnotic. It has me confessing my deepest, darkest desires to him before I can talk myself out of it. His wicked demands and erotic words make me want to obey his every command.

And those words...Jesus, what those words do to me! Just the thought of hearing his voice on the other end of the line each night leaves me dripping wet in anticipation.

"Well?" Autumn Romano finally demands, her tone rife with impatience. "How did it go?"

"Three," I say.

Lola Knight's blue eyes widened in shock. "Three? From *phone sex*?"

"Good god," Autumn mouths.

I nod, easing myself down to the table.

"Good?" Lola asks.

"Toe-curling, couldn't feel my legs afterward good," I whisper, blushing.

"Good grief," Autumn says, awe in her tone. "Brilliant man."

I bob my head in silent agreement. Tex is definitely brilliant. And wicked. And sexy as hell. And a thousand different things I crave more than I know how to put into words.

"Any more hints about who he is?" Lola asks.

"No." I shake my head, frowning. "But I'm telling you, he's Granger. The voice is the same, and the way he says my name is the same. Even the way he talks to me...it's like he knows what I look like." It's all of that and more. I'm convinced the man in charge of our roofing crew is Tex. I can't even pinpoint what makes me so certain. I just *know* it's him with unshakable certainty.

Unfortunately, he hasn't once indicated he wants me to know. And it's not exactly something I can bring up. Even if I weren't contractually obligated not to approach a client, an "oh, by the way, I'm a phone sex operator. Do you happen to call 1-900-Do-Arwen every night and have amazing phone sex with me?" doesn't exactly roll off the tongue.

"Our ridiculously hot roofer is a phone sex virtuoso," Autumn says, blinking her brown eyes.

The man is gorgeous. He's all blond hair, green eyes, and golden skin over acres of brawny muscles. He's older than we are by at least a decade, but I'm so attracted to him that it's ridiculous. Hell, I'm pretty sure I'm in love with him. He's always so sweet to me. He brings me breakfast most mornings and always takes time to ask me about my classes. Even though we're on summer break, I have a full schedule like always. I'm kind of nerdy like that. But he doesn't mind. He listens when I ramble on about everything under the sun, remembers what I like and don't like, and never makes fun of me. He's respectful, kind, and funny. And he's so damn protective! He gets grumpy when the other roofers try to talk to me.

But I don't know if he feels the same way I do. Sometimes, he looks at me, and I think he does. But he hasn't made a move. He keeps our relationship professional when he's here and anything but when he calls each night. Yet he didn't even give me his real name on the phone. That isn't a sign that he wants me to know it's him calling. For all I know, he doesn't even know I'm the Arwen getting him off every night.

Surely, he does, though, right? I mean, there aren't that many of us. Maybe he thinks the name is just coincidental because it's so uncommon. Does he believe the girl he talks to on the phone at night picked it like a stage name?

I sigh in frustration and lay my head down on the table, as uncertain as ever.

"He'll be here soon," Autumn says. "Maybe it's time you take matters into your own hands."

"How's she going to do that?" Lola asks. "You know she can't just confront him. Client privacy rules forbid it. Besides, what if she does and she's wrong?"

This is precisely why I haven't approached him already. I would be completely mortified if I asked him if he calls me every night, only to find out that he doesn't. I'm not ashamed of the work. Sex work and sex workers deserve respect just like everyone else. But I don't want to offend him. And I really don't want to find out that I'm wrong.

I *need* Tex and Granger to be the same person because I can't be in love with two different people. It'll break my heart into a million tiny pieces. But why the hell would someone like Granger need to call someone like me for phone sex? I'm a curvy virgin. He's older, hotter, and successful. Every woman here stares at him when he's working. He could have anyone!

"I know," Autumn says. "But he obviously likes her if he's calling her every night."

"So says you," I mutter, finally lifting my head from the table to face my best friends again. They're both eyeing me, Lola in worry and Autumn with a distinct gleam in her eyes. I love them both to death, but they couldn't be more opposite. I'm surprised Autumn is the one pushing me to make a move. She doesn't trust easily—or at all—when it comes to men. Her dad was not a good guy, and his friends were even worse.

I'm sad she's moving back to Silver Spoon Falls, Texas. I'm going to miss her desperately.

"Trust me," Autumn says, "he wants you. I saw how that man looked at you Monday when you were out by the pool."

"She's right," Lola says. "Granger is wild about you, Arwen."

"So what am I supposed to do about it?" I groan. "Like you said, I can't confront him and ask if he gives me mind-blowing orgasms over the phone!"

"Then don't approach him." Autumn shrugs a shoulder. "Make him come to you."

"How?" I'm more than willing to listen to any advice here. I'm going insane! Granger and his crew will be finished with the roof of our building in a day or two at the most. Time is running out.

Autumn drums her fingers against the table, her brows furrowed in thought. "Take tonight off work. When he gets here tomorrow, flag him down and tell him you're expecting a phone call, but you need to shower. Ask if he minds grabbing it for you when it rings. Tell him it's a very important call." She waves her hand as if to say *be creative.* "I'll have Emma call to confirm an appointment at the spa for you and make sure she lets it slip just exactly what kind of appointment it is."

Lola throws her head back and laughs. "Brilliant! Make him think she's getting a wax for a hot date. He'll be chomping at the bit if he's your Tex."

"Maybe," I say doubtfully. "What happens when he calls tomorrow night, and I'm not on said date?"

"You aren't working tomorrow night, either." Autumn brings her coffee mug to her lips and takes a sip before continuing, "Call your boss and tell her you're taking the rest of the week off."

"And if this backfires?" I demand. "If he thinks I'm seeing someone else, he might run the other way."

"Please," Autumn scoffs. "You've told us the things that man says to you. He doesn't play well with others, Arwen. If he thinks you're going out with someone else, he'll step up and put a stop to it."

I eye her doubtfully, knowing full well that her plans don't always work the way she expects. The fact that she has a criminal record is proof of that. She's been arrested twice for protesting. I'm pretty sure she was protesting her own family's company both times.

"Pretend you aren't certain about the date," Lola advises, more reserved than Autumn. "Tell him we set it up for you, but you figure it's time to put yourself out there and find someone, so you're going for it."

"Yes!" Autumn claps her hands.

I consider their insane plan. It could work. From everything I know about Tex or Granger, he's possessive. But he's also the kind of man who asks if I'm okay before ending our calls each night and the type of guy who cautions me to watch out for nails every time I step outside in flip-flops. Autumn's plan will appeal to the former side, with Lola's additions appealing to the latter. If Granger really is Tex, this might actually force him out into the open once and for all.

And if he isn't Tex? a little voice whispers.

Well, I'll just have to cross that hurdle when I get to it.

Please, please don't let me get to it, I pray.

"Let's do it," I say, my decision made.

Chapter Three

Granger

I brought you something.

I glance up from the bed of my truck to see Arwen standing on the sidewalk, shielding her eyes against the sun. The strap of her sundress slips down her left shoulder, making my fucking mouth water. I want to taste her skin right where the sun hits it.

"Yeah? And what did you bring me?" I ask, my eyes prowling all over her curvy body. God have mercy. She's too pretty for words, smiling at me like she knows a secret I don't.

Her hands slip from behind her back. "This," she says, presenting a cupcake to me.

My stomach growls. Not for the food. For her. I want to lick the frosting off her naked body.

"You're always bringing me food. I figured it was my turn." She steps off the sidewalk, presenting the cupcake to me. The damn thing is bigger than her delicate little hand. "It's strawberry cheesecake flavored."

I wrap my hand around her wrist, holding her steady as I take the cupcake from her. She shivers at my touch, her nipples turning to hard points in her dress.

"What did you do last night, little one?"

A tiny smile curves her plump lips upward, a blush staining her cheeks. "Nothing," she whispers, the pulse in her throat jumping. "Just work."

"Mm."

Did you dream about me after you passed out last night, baby doll?

I peel the wrapper from the cupcake, bringing it to my lips before I can ask that question. Fucking hell. If I don't find a way out of my own misery soon, I'm going to start ripping shit apart. Starting with her fucking roof so I have an excuse to drag this job out for as long as possible.

"What did you do?" she asks.

"Same thing I do every night."

I called you. You cried out for me while you fucked yourself on your fingers.

"Oh." Her teeth sink into her bottom lip, and then her eyes flash to mine. "Well, I hope you enjoyed it."

I meet her gaze, holding it captive. "I *always* enjoy it, Arwen."

She shivers again.

"Yo, boss!"

I whip my head around, staring daggers at the apprentice shouting my name from across the parking lot. He clearly can't take a fucking hint because he lifts his hand in a wave, motioning me over.

"Well, I should let you get back to work," Arwen says, stepping back onto the sidewalk. I suddenly want to strangle my apprentice. "Bye, Granger."

"Talk to you later, little one," I promise.

"I'm sorry. Arwen isn't accepting calls tonight."

"What the fuck?" I growl, stabbing the button to end the call as the automated message replays for the third time. Why isn't she taking calls? She always works on Wednesdays. Hell, she's worked every damn night since she started the job.

I pick up my cell, tapping out a text before I can talk myself out of it. She gave me her number when I needed access to their attic. I haven't used it since my third day on the job, but I've already broke every other rule when it comes to her. Might as well break this one too.

Me: Thank you for the cupcake today.

I want to ask why she isn't taking calls tonight but don't. There will be no convincing her I'm not a goddamn creep, then. No more cupcakes or sweet smiles. I'll be kicked out of her life fast enough to make my head spin.

The thought makes me sick to my stomach. I'm not just obsessed with Arwen. I'm fucking wild about her. I fell in love the second I set eyes on her, and I've only fallen deeper every moment since then. I don't just want to fuck her. I want to be the center of her world. And I want to make her the center of mine. She won't want for anything, won't need anything. I'll work like a goddamn dog to make her happy.

Arwen: You're welcome.

I hesitate for a moment and then say screw it and ask what I really want to know.

Me: What are you doing tonight?

I drum my fingers on the bed beside me, impatiently waiting for a response. Jesus. If she's out with some other man, I'm going to lose my mind. A growl rumbles in my throat, possessive jealousy churning through me. She better not be out with another man.

She's mine. She has been since I met her. I just need to figure out how to convince her that I'm not a complete asshole.

Arwen: The same thing I do every night.

"Little liar," I mumble, reading her texts. She isn't doing what she does every night. If she were, we'd be on the phone right now, and she'd be well on her way to her third orgasm. Fuck. Unless she means she's *already* on her way to her third orgasm. Is my girl touching my pussy? Without me?

Hell no. Her orgasms belong to me.

Me: Don't work yourself too hard, little one. You won't have any energy left for the best moments in life. It'd be a damn shame for you to miss something incredible because you're keeping yourself too busy.

I smirk at the message. If she has an inkling of who I am, she'll know exactly what I mean. And if she doesn't know I'm Tex, hopefully, it'll make her think of the moments he gives her. Either way, I have a feeling she won't find getting off by herself nearly as much fun after she reads it.

Three little dots pop up on the screen as she starts typing and then stops, only to start again. She does this four times in a row before the three dots vanish.

Me: Sweet dreams, Arwen.

Arwen: Goodnight, Granger.

I smile and set my phone aside. One way or another, I'm making this girl mine.

Chapter Four

Arwen

"Granger texted me last night."

"Of course he did," Autumn says, carrying a mug of coffee to the table. "He probably flipped his lid as soon as he realized you weren't working."

Lola laughs quietly, slathering butter on a piece of toast. "He's got it so bad for you."

"What did he say."

"He thanked me for the cupcake I bought him yesterday." I drop a pod into the Keurig and then stick my mug beneath, and hit the button before turning to face my best friends. "And then he asked what I was doing."

"Of course he did." Autumn sighs dramatically. "Do you need more proof that he's Tex?"

"No," I say slowly, shaking my head. Between our conversation yesterday and his texts last night, I'm more certain than ever that my crazy-hot roofer is the same man who has been calling me every night. "I think he's been calling me on purpose."

"Uh, clearly!" Lola cries, an amused smile lighting up her face.

Autumn's brows furrow.

"No way!" I cry as soon as I see them wrinkle. "Don't even say it."

"I wasn't going to say it," she mumbles.

Lola snorts.

"I wasn't," Autumn protests. She doesn't trust easily, especially not men. It makes her overprotective and suspicious of everyone. I love her to death for it, but Granger isn't one of her dad's creepy friends. I don't know why he started calling me instead of asking me out. Maybe some people would find it inappropriate, but I find it kind of...hot.

We got to know each other in a way most people don't. With our identities hidden, we were stripped bare. He knows things about me no one else knows. My deepest desires. My darkest fantasies. I know the same about him. I don't regret that.

Now, I want both sides of him at the same time. I don't want Granger by day and Tex by night. I want every piece of him all the time. And I want him to have every piece of me the same way. No more hiding behind a 1-900 number.

Today, I'm declaring war.

"Hey, Granger," I say, trying not to stare as he steps inside our apartment two hours later, his tool belt around his jean-clad hips, nothing but a white tank covering his torso. His tattooed arms are bare, lines of ink running across the solid muscle. His hair is wild, his jaw scruffy. He looks edible.

"Arwen," he growls, his green eyes flaring with heat as they rake down my body. I'm in nothing but a lingerie robe and a pair of slippers. The robe ends at mid-thigh, leaving my legs completely bare. It's more than I wear sunbathing by the pool, but usually by the time he arrives, I'm in full grad-student gear, ready for class.

"Sorry," I say, blushing as his eyes linger on my legs. "I'm running behind this morning."

"Busy night?" he asks, cocking his head to the side. Mischievous lights gleam in his eyes, almost wicked in their intensity.

My lips curve into a small, mysterious smile in response. He just has to be Tex!

"I need a huge favor from you," I blurt, ready to get on with it.

He nods for me to continue, his eyes riveted on my face. He watches me so intently, as if he's hanging onto every word. I love it so much.

"I'm expecting a call from the spa. Would you mind hanging around inside for a bit in case they call while I'm in the shower? Autumn is heading out, Lola's already off at work, and I don't want to miss it." I plead with wide, innocent eyes, hoping he doesn't tell me no. Technically, he's not supposed to be in here at all. But he's been breaking the rules since he started this job. He doesn't let his crew get away with breaking them though. They aren't allowed to stick a single toe over our threshold.

"Sure thing," he drawls, dipping his head a little in that charming, sexy way of his.

I beam at him and then let my shoulders fall.

"I can't believe I let the girls talk me into this," I mutter under my breath, only partially pretending. Lying to him feels wrong, even though my lie is tiny compared to his. I'm not very good at it. My dad always says I'm too much like my mom. She's not very good at lying either.

"What are they plottin' now?" Granger asks, taking the bait even though a big part of me wishes he wouldn't.

"Oh. They've decided I need to get out from beneath the books for a while and have a little fun. They've set me up on a date tonight." I don't miss the way his eyes immediately narrow, his body tensing. I bravely press on. "I don't really know why I'm complaining. They're right.

I haven't had a date in...well, longer than I care to admit." I laugh self-consciously, not willing to admit to this man just how long it's actually been. "I just..."

"Just what?" he growls, crossing his arms and leaning back against the front door.

"I just..." I huff and then hurry on with the speech I rehearsed in front of Lola and Autumn earlier. "I don't know. I'm just not sure this is going to be any fun. The guy's an accountant. Not exactly my type."

It's true. Granger is my type. He's charming and bossy and sweet and filthy and all those things at once. Plus, I grew up with a cop for a father and an army of overprotective uncles right next door. I didn't date. I couldn't because everyone was too afraid of my dad and uncles and brothers. It was the same way for my cousins. If a guy can't handle them, he can't handle me. Most guys can't handle them.

Granger though? I already know Granger wouldn't let them boss him around or run him off. He wouldn't take any crap. He's an alpha just like they are. He gives the orders and expects to be obeyed. I love that about him. He won't back down when it comes to me. That's what I want. Someone willing to fight for me. Not someone who does what he's told.

"What is your type?" Granger asks.

"I like a man who isn't afraid to take charge or get a little dirty." I leave it up to him to decide what I mean by that. "Someone not afraid to do something completely unexpected or spontaneous."

"You like bad boys," Granger says, speculation in his tone.

"Maybe. They can keep up." I think it would be very boring to live life inside the lines.

"And accountants can't?" he asks, his lips curling into an amused smile.

"Probably not," I say.

"Ditch the accountant," he growls, his eyes locked on mine. It's not a suggestion, not really. The look in his eyes makes it clear this is a demand. "You can do better."

"Can I?" I ask, my gaze sweeping across his form before I shrug. "No one else is interested. I might as well give the accountant a chance. Who knows? Maybe he'll surprise me."

With that, I turn on my heel and start up the stairs, adding a little extra sway for his benefit.

It might be my imagination, but I think I hear him growl behind me.

Chapter Five

Granger

"**S**on of a bitch," I curse, watching as Arwen climbs the stairs, her robe riding up her thighs to reveal even more of those gorgeous legs to my gaze. She's going out with someone else. Someone who, clearly, doesn't get her or what she needs. *Someone who isn't me.*

Hell no.

Leaning my head back against the wall, I groan loudly. The thought of letting her go out with someone else, with *anyone* else, has my possessive side roaring for blood. She's mine. I'm not letting her go out with anyone else. Not today or any other day.

"You like her."

I peel my eyes open to find Autumn Romano standing in the doorway between the living room and kitchen, eyeing me with a gleam in her dark eyes. Like Arwen, she's a smart girl. But Arwen is innocent in every sense of the word. She sees the best in everyone. Autumn is different. She's been through things that make her see the world a little more clearly. I don't think she trusts me.

"You've been calling her every night, haven't you?" she demands.

Well, fuck.

I freeze like a deer caught in the headlights...not exactly a feeling I'm used to. But then again, I've never been in a situation like this before either. If I tell Autumn the truth, she might kick my ass out the door before I can explain. She's far more intimidating than the petite beauty wreaking havoc on my credit card bill. She's also protective as hell.

"I don't know what game you're playing, but if you hurt her, I will kill you."

"I don't want to hurt her," I say, holding up my hands. Might as well sort that out now. "Hell, Autumn, I don't even know what I'm doing."

"Not enough, clearly," she sniffs, crossing her arms and hitting me with a haughty glare. "She knows it's you."

"Why hasn't she said anything?" I demand, stunned at that revelation. Arwen already knows I'm Tex? Christ Almighty. And she hasn't bludgeoned me with a stiletto? Or worse, called the cops and reported me for stalking?

"Client privacy. She can't approach you, but she wants to."

Fuck me. My baby doll wants me? Even knowing what I've been doing?

"Why are you telling me this?" I ask, knowing full well Autumn wouldn't let me anywhere near Arwen if she thought I was a stalker or a creep or a pervert or any of the fifty other things this situation makes me out to be.

"Because you'll be finished here in two days, and she's driving herself insane trying to figure out how to get you to tell her the truth." Autumn rolls her eyes. "You've really messed this up."

"I know. I didn't intend for it to happen."

"Yeah, well, it did." Her sympathetic expression softens her blunt response. "I don't want to know how you found out about her job or why you decided to call instead of asking her out, but if you want her, I suggest you go after her. She isn't going to keep this gig forever, you know. Another week or two, and she'll be done with the hotline for good."

Shit.

"She has a date."

Autumn laughs, arching a brow. "Afraid of a little ole accountant, Granger? Maybe you aren't right for her after all."

Even knowing she's just trying to get a rise out of me, I grunt, narrowing my eyes. Like hell I'm intimidated by an accountant. Arwen's mine, even if she doesn't know it yet.

"I'm right for her," I say, daring Autumn to disagree. She may have known Arwen longer, but I know her in ways Autumn never will. I know exactly how right for her I can be. And I know Arwen feels it too. She wouldn't still let me in here if she didn't.

"Then I suggest you do something about it." Autumn snags her purse from the back of the couch. "Wouldn't want the accountant to steal her from you, would you?" she calls over her shoulder as she heads back into the kitchen.

I stand at the bottom of the stairs for a long moment, staring up at Arwen's closed door. Autumn's advice rings in my ears, taunting me. If there's even a chance she's right...I'm taking it. I have to take it. Arwen's mine.

Chapter Six

Arwen

I pace restlessly around my bedroom, waiting for the phone to ring. I'm nervous that this is a bad idea and that it'll blow up in my face, but I'm committed now. Seeing it through is all I can do at this point. But I cannot even begin to describe how much I don't want to be wrong. The thought of Granger and Tex being two entirely different people makes my stomach quiver and churn.

I can't be that wrong, can I?

God, I hope not.

The only reason I've even fallen for Tex is *because* I'm so sure he's Granger. Phone sex isn't exactly a solid foundation for a relationship. But Tex is the side of Granger no one else gets to see. I like thinking I'm the only one who gets that part of him. I like thinking that he calls me because he wants to give me that part of him. I don't want it to be a coincidence or accident or anything less than intentional.

Maybe that makes me crazy. But it's how I feel.

The phone rings.

"Oh, shoot," I whisper, holding my breath as it rings again and then again.

It cuts off abruptly halfway through the fourth ring.

I expel a heavy breath, relieved Granger answered it, even as knots form in my stomach. He's talking to Emma now, hearing all about the fake Brazilian wax I'm about to have done for a hot date I don't have. He's either jotting the message down in disinterest...or growing hot under the collar.

"Please, please, please," I chant quietly before heading toward the adjoining bathroom to shower. I strip quickly and adjust the water before stepping beneath the spray and allowing the warm water to beat down on me. My thoughts race in circles, but I do my best to tune them out.

Miraculously, the hot water helps clear my mind and calm my racing heart.

By the time I step from the shower, I feel calmer. I hum a little as I wrap the towel around me and step back into my room to dress.

"We need to talk."

I scream as Granger's voice sounds from across the room. I whip my head in that direction to find him leaning against the bedroom door like some angry cowboy, his thumbs hooked into his jean pockets, and his jaw clenched.

"Granger," I squeak and then clear my throat. "You scared me."

"Sorry, baby doll." He dips his head in that sexy, charming way of his.

"W-what are you doing in here?"

"Hopin' you don't kick my ass," he drawls, pushing away from the door and stepping toward me. His eyes lock with mine, so dark green they make me dizzy. "The spa called. Emma said she can fit you in as soon as you can get there."

"Okay." I lick my lips, nervous as hell.

"I told her you'd be there tomorrow." He takes another step toward me.

"To...what?"

"Tomorrow," he repeats, moving closer. "As in, not today."

I swallow hard, not sure what to think.

Is this a good thing?

Is it a bad thing?

Why is he in my room waiting for me?

Why isn't he naked in my room waiting for me?

"Why tomorrow?" I manage to ask. The question is a mere breath, not at all confident or seductive or any other such thing. I sound as nervous as I feel.

"You don't want to go out with the accountant tonight, Arwen," he says, taking another step toward me. He's so close; all I'd have to do is lean forward an inch, and I'd be in his arms. He reaches out and tilts my face up with a finger beneath my chin. "The accountant doesn't know what you want."

The wicked, devilish look in his eyes is exactly how I imagine he looks at me when Tex is whispering to me over the phone.

"He doesn't?"

Granger shakes his head, silent.

"What——" I have to clear my throat to force out sound. "What are you doing in here?"

"I talked to Autumn."

"Autumn," I repeat.

"I'm not stalking you," he says, his green eyes burning with sincerity.

"Okay...?" My heart pounds double time now. I'm half afraid of where this conversation seems to be heading and half ready to scream in triumph at where I hope it's headed.

"I heard you talking to her and Lola my first day here," Granger murmurs, still cupping my chin lightly in his hand, forcing me to look at him. "You were tellin' them how nervous you were about your new job, and how you didn't think you'd be any good at it since you're still a virgin."

Oh God, he heard that?

"You sounded so nervous and looked so fucking perfect," he whispers. "The thought of some other man giving you that first sexual experience made me crazy, little one. I wanted it to be me so fuckin' bad." He swallows hard. "So I called you."

Relief pours through me in a flood, weakening my knees. I have to lock them to remain upright.

"You asked for my name, and I realized how bad it would sound if I told you who I really was, so I made up a name."

"Wh–what name?" I ask even though I already know.

"Tex," he states.

Blood rushes in my ears at his confirmation. He's really Tex.

"I told myself I was only going to call you once," he continues before I manage to put thoughts together in anything resembling a cohesive manner. "But I was lyin' to myself, Arwen. I tried to stop after that first night, but I couldn't let anyone else talk to you like that."

"Why not?" I whisper.

"Because I'm crazy about you, little one." His eyes glow with sincerity and with something darker. Possession. Jealousy. "When I saw you glowing the next morning, I knew I couldn't let anyone else be the reason for that. It *had* to be me. So I called again. And I kept callin'."

I open my mouth and then snap it closed, not a single word coming to mind. He's stolen all of them. My heart pounds against my breastbone, butterflies dancing a ballet in my stomach.

"I fucking love being the reason you have that look in your eye every day." He swallows hard. "I should have told you the truth. I'm an asshole for not telling you the truth. I didn't want you to hate me."

"I don't hate you," I whisper. How can I? Every single night, he made it about me. I'm not sure he if ever even allowed himself to orgasm from our calls. If so, I never heard him. He was always focused on pleasing me.

"I'm sorry I didn't tell you, but you should know I don't regret callin' you." He blows out a breath. "If you want to kick my ass for it, I won't stop you."

"I don't want that," I say, quickly shaking my head. I want him. Short of throwing myself into his arms, I'm not sure how to tell him that, though. I've never had a hard time finding words, but this is different. *Granger* is different.

"You're not mad?"

I shake my head, completely mute.

He searches my face, his brows furrowed, eyes narrowed and focused. Whatever he finds in my expression seems to reassure him. His eyes darken, his rigid stance loosening.

"I'm going to kiss you now," he says.

"Please," I sob.

The last vestiges of worry in his eyes vanish, leaving nothing but wicked intent in their place. He snakes an arm around my waist, pulling me up against him.

His lips descended on mine, his kiss warm and soft.

"Open for me, sweetheart," he demands, flicking his tongue against my bottom lip.

I obey his request, pressing my mouth to his and allowing him inside. He cups the back of my neck, angling my head as he deepens the kiss, his tongue sliding sinuously against mine.

"Mm," he groans into my mouth, pulling me closer as my knees buckle.

I gasp, feeling him everywhere. He feels even better than I imagined he would, hard muscles molding to my softer curves in all the right places. My mind spins from his kiss. It's steam and cinnamon coursing through my veins like a shot of adrenaline.

He pulls back slowly, running his lips along my jaw and onto my throat. His words from the night before echo in my mind, pulling a moan from my lips at the thought of him marking me. I want him to do it. Desperately.

"Granger, please. I want you."

"Are you wet for me, Arwen?" he breathes against my ear, his hands moving to the folds of my towel.

"Yes," I whisper as he rakes his teeth across my throat. Shards of pleasure lance through me, threatening to unmake me. This is really happening. Granger is Tex, and he's really here.

The towel slides from my body, leaving me bare to his questing hands. They work in counterpoint to his mouth—soft lips at my throat, big, rough hands gliding across my damp skin.

My hands land against his broad shoulders, steadying me as he brushes across my nipples and palms my breasts. His mouth follows, pulling first one and then the other nipple between his lips and sucking hard.

I cry out in pleasure at the deep draw of his mouth.

"I know what you need," he croons, lifting his head and urging me back toward my bed. "I know how you need it. Let me give it to you."

I nod willingly, allowing him to draw me down to the bed. My eyes lock on his face as he stares down at me, his expression ravenous. Each sweep of his eyes across my body have me writhing atop the bed. I don't have to ask to know he finds me beautiful. It's written right there on his face.

"Spread your legs and let me see that pretty pussy, baby doll," he murmurs. "Let me see how wet you are for me."

My legs fall open slowly, exposing me to the man who already knows my body so well. He coaxed my deepest desires from me with nothing more than words whispered through the telephone. Learned every fantasy I have with little more than sinful questions and soft growls of satisfaction at each answer willingly given. The thought of him putting that knowledge to use has me more worked up now than I ever was over the phone.

His gaze rakes down my body again, leaving little fires in their wake. "Yes," he groans when his heated gaze finally settles between my legs. He reaches out slowly and runs a thick finger through my soaked folds. "So goddamn wet," he murmurs, bringing his finger to his lips to taste me.

I writhe when he growls and sucks his finger clean.

"I'm going to make you taste like me before you leave this bed, Arwen," he says. The erotic promise echoes in his eyes. "I'm going to fuck you hard, just like you need, little one. Are you on birth control?"

"No."

"If you don't want my kid, you better tell me now, sweetheart," he says. "Otherwise, I'll be breeding you when I pop that cherry."

"I..." Oh my gosh. Is it wrong how badly I want that?

"Yeah, you want it," he says with a chuckle.

"Please," I whimper. I don't care if it's wrong. I want it. I'm dying to feel him inside of me, bare. Breeding me. I've wanted it for days already. I'm tired of waiting.

"First, I'm going to make you come on my tongue." He drops to his knees at the edge of the bed and grasps my hips, dragging me forward until my ass hangs off the bed.

I moan at his touch—not too gentle and not too rough.

"I've wanted this since you opened the door that first morning." He drapes my thighs brazenly across his broad shoulders and blows on my clit. I nearly come unglued at the sensation. "I wanted to make you scream for me." His eyes meet mine again as he leans forward and inhales deeply. "Scream for me now, little one," he growls, burying his face between my thighs.

His tongue does to me what his words did over the phone. Only it's a thousand times better. He devours me, plunging his tongue deep and then pulling back to suck my clit into his mouth. His hands are like vises on my hips, digging into the flesh of my ass and spreading me wide open for him.

I've never felt so exposed or so good before. The way he uses his tongue is art. Just as he demanded, I scream for him. I scream until my throat is raw and an intense orgasm shatters me apart like finely blown glass. It's incredible.

His fingers join his tongue then, manipulating my body like a familiar instrument. The symphony he plays against my folds goes on and on, leaving me breathless. When his eyes meet mine again, he grins, his green eyes nearly black with lust.

"I like the way you scream my name," he murmurs, rising to his feet with me in his arms. He carefully lays me on the bed before tugging his shirt off over his head. The lines of ink on his arms are etched across his pecs too. Reds and blacks dip and swirl against his golden skin until the dragon inked there seems to move with the muscle beneath. He's hard and taut everywhere, his years as a roofer having molded his body into lithe, powerful muscle.

"You like the ink," he says, as he undoes the tool belt and lets it drop to the floor with a thud. He isn't asking. His words are a simple statement of fact. "You really do like the bad boys, don't you?"

I can't make my mouth work well enough to form an answer. I'm still dazed, the two orgasms leaving my entire body feeling hazy and insubstantial. All I can do is stare at him. But it's not bad boys I like. It's him.

He undresses with steady hands, not cocky at what he reveals to me, but confident with what he reveals to me. I can't look away. He's breathtaking. His pants drop slowly, his cock springing free.

"Oh," I mouth, desire breaking through the post-orgasmic haze and sending another rush of arousal flooding between my legs. His cock is long and thick, jutting proudly from his body. He's so hard, the bulbous head purple and glistening with pre-cum, his balls tight beneath.

"Look at it, Arwen," he demands, wrapping his hand around that beautiful cock and pumping. "Imagine how I'm going to feel inside of you. How tight you're going to feel stretched around my cock. Do you want it, little one?"

"Yes," I whisper, arching against the bed in anticipation.

He crawls onto the bed above me, urging my legs apart. "I want to see you when I fuck you, sweetheart," he whispers, leaning down to pull my nipple into his mouth. He bites gently and then tugs with his teeth before releasing it. "I want to watch your face when you come on my cock for the first time."

I moan loudly and writhe against him.

He hitches my leg around his hip and guides himself to my entrance. "Open your eyes," he croons as his tip nudges my entrance. "Watch me while I fill you."

My eyes flew open wide, locking on his face as he begins to press himself inside of me. He does it slowly, stretching me inch by inch. There's a brief flash of pain when my virgin barrier tears, but as soon as I tense, he kisses me, and I forget all about it. By the time he lets me up for air, the pain is gone.

He sheathes himself inside me in one deep thrust then. His head kicks back on his shoulders, a pleased growl tearing from his lips. The expression on his face is captivating. It's pleasure and pain, desire and need.

I know my own matches. I've never felt so full, stretched wide around his thick cock. It's overwhelmingly perfect. I want to cry with the pleasure of it. I lay still instead, savoring the way he feels inside me, on top of me.

"I'm going to fuck you now, Arwen," he whispers, easing himself out. "Hard."

"Oh God," I whimper, my stomach muscles contracting.

"My name is Granger, little one. Scream it for me," he murmurs, and begins to move. He goes slow at first, letting me get used to the way he feels. Within moments, I'm pleading for more. I don't want him to hold back or take it easy on me. I'm not delicate.

"More," I gasp, writhing beneath him. "More."

He growls and fucks me harder, his powerful thrusts driving his cock into me hard and fast. "Feel it, Arwen," he groans between hard, driving strikes. "Feel what I can do to you. Your accountant couldn't do this, little one. He doesn't know what you need. He doesn't know how to take care of you like I do."

I moan loudly in response, unable to find the words to tell him there is no accountant.

"He doesn't know how dirty you can be," he grunts, adjusting his hold on my hip. It allows him to drive deeper. The bed rocks and groans beneath us. I don't care. I'm in heaven, crying out in bliss with every thrust. "I know though. I know just how to make you come undone."

"Yes," I groan, rocking with him. The slap of his balls against my ass stings in just the right way. I feel alive like I never have before. The way my heart pounds in my chest. The way Granger feels above me. The sounds of his grunts and the scent of sex in the air. It all seems to brand me like a physical mark on my skin making me his. His to touch. His to fuck. His to please.

"Come for me, Arwen," he growls, leaning down over me. "I want to feel your juices on my cock." He sinks his teeth lightly into the dip between my neck and shoulder, sucking my flesh into his mouth.

His bite is pleasure and pain, and exactly the mark he promised would let the world know I belong to him. I cry out his name as he goes wild above me, pounding into me without rhythm. He groans into my neck as my inner muscles flutter around him, and I come undone.

"Little one," he cries out, falling still above me. His cock jerks hard inside of me as he releases inside me, filling me full of him.

I fall limp beneath him, blood rushing in my ears and his sweat dripping onto my skin.

"Granger," I breathe, aftershocks still quaking through me. "There is no accountant."

"Thank God," he says, slipping out of me. His cum dribbles out. He growls when he sees it and scoops it up on his fingers. "This stays inside you."

"Oh my God," I moan, writhing as he pushes it back inside me. His thumb brushes over my clit.

"Fuck, I love the sight of you like this," he mutters, rolling to his side and dragging me into his arms. "It sure as hell beats listening to you hang up."

"You wait for me to hang up?"

"Every damn night," he growls.

"I want to take you out tonight," Granger announces, pulling his pants on.

"Yeah?" I ask, sitting up in the bed and pulling the sheet up around me, smiling. I'm still dazed, and completely sated from the intense way he made love to me. I lost count of how many times he made me come with his fingers and his mouth before reluctantly dragging himself out of bed.

"Yeah," he says, grinning at me. "Will you come?"

"You know I will," I say quietly. There's no doubt about that whatsoever. Granger, Tex...it doesn't matter what name he uses. I'll go anywhere he wants to take me.

"Good." He pulls his wife beater back over his head before leaning over me. His mouth descends on mine briefly, his kiss hot and hard. "Be ready at seven, little one."

"Okay."

"I'm sorry I didn't tell you earlier," he murmurs, wrapping a wayward curl around his finger.

"It's okay," I assure him, holding his gaze. "I'm just glad you did tell me."

"Me too," he says, grinning again. "You're fucking perfect, and not just when you're coming for me either. I hope you're ready for me, Arwen Grayson. I'm going to make you fall in love with me." With that, he picks up his tool belt and heads toward the door. "Marriage, babies. I want it all, little one."

"Hey, Granger?" I call, my heart turning somersaults in my chest.

He turns back to me, grinning. "Yeah, little one?"

"Call me anytime," I say with a wink.

"Oh, I plan on it," he promises, his eyes gleaming with wicked intent.

I flop back down on the bed, a smile plastered across my face. He's not going to have to try very hard to get me to fall in love with him considering that I'm already there. We're moving at the speed of light, but it just feels...right. Everything about him feels right. Better than that. It feels perfect.

Within seconds of the front door closing downstairs, my cell phone rings. I grab for it, the name on the display sending butterflies dancing through my stomach. I grin and swipe to answer. "Hi, this is Arwen..."

"Hello, Arwen, this is Granger," he murmurs.

"Hello, Granger." I laugh in delight, my heart rolling in my chest.

"You're naked for me, aren't you?" he asks.

"You could always come back up here and find out," I tease, snuggling up beneath the blankets that now smell like him.

The front door opens again.

"Little one," Granger calls from downstairs.

My smile grows so big it nearly splits my cheeks.

No, he's not going to have to try very hard at all.

Chapter Seven

Granger

"**H**ey, baby. It's Arwen."

I grip the phone tightly in my hand as her sweet voice whispers down the line. Desire stirs, hitting me like a fist at the breathless hitch in her voice. Every word I meant to say leaves my mind in an instant. The only thing left behind is burning hunger and the need to hear her come undone for me one more time.

"I need you naked," I growl.

"Oh, yeah? Then maybe you should come and do something about that," she says.

I grind my palm against my cock, laying my head back against the seat of my truck. "I would, but then we'd have a problem."

"You naked is never a problem in my book, Granger."

I chuckle, fighting the urge to pull my cock out right in the middle of her fucking parking lot to relieve the pressure. She's hot enough to tempt a saint, and I've never been one of those. Hell, when it comes to her, I'm barely even a gentleman. But I'm not going inside until I say what I need to say.

If I do, I'll have her naked and beneath me before we talk. And I don't want to wait to have this conversation. It's waited too damn long already.

"I have something to tell you, little one."

"You're finished with the roof," she whispers.

"Yeah, we're finished." We finished yesterday, but I stuck around today to make damn sure it was perfect. Any excuse to be close to her for a little while longer.

"What happens now?"

"That's what I wanted to talk to you about."

"Oh."

"Move in with me," I blurt. I've been thinking about it non-fucking-stop. I'm not ready to not see her every day. Truth is, I won't ever be prepared not to see her every day. I'm in love with this woman and won't anything change that. I don't need time to know how I feel about her. I know it now. I knew it before the first time we fucked. The last week has only confirmed what I knew then. She owns me, body and soul.

"You want me to move in with you?"

"Fuck yes," I growl. "Been thinkin' about it all week, little one."

"Granger, is this because you won't be here every day anymore?"

The door of her apartment flies open. She steps outside, her dark curls loose around her face, and the phone clutched at her ear. She's dressed in a silk robe, the belt cinched tight around her waist. Every inch of her creamy legs is visible. Like always, I lose the ability to think straight as soon as I set eyes on her.

I climb from the truck, pulled toward her as if a magnet connects the two of us.

"Move in with me," I whisper, stopping in front of her.

"We're still on the phone."

"I know. I'm tryin' to keep my hands off of you."

"Oh." Her brows furrow. "Why?"

"Because I've got somethin' else to say, and if I get my hands on you, it'll be a while before either of us say anything that doesn't end in moaning."

Her cheeks heat, a pretty blush stealing across them as her gaze roves over my face.

"I'm wild about you, Arwen Grayson. I've been in love with you since I first set eyes on you," I say to her, the phone still clutched in my fist. "That's why I need you to move in with me. Not because I won't be here every day, but because it's where you belong."

"Granger."

"I know you feel the same way." I ditch the phone, shoving it into my pocket to reach for her. "You say it in your sleep. You love me, little one."

"So much," she whispers, her big blue eyes wide.

Mine fall closed, my heart threatening to beat out of my fucking chest. Jesus. We're going to have to name one of our kids after Autumn. She gave me the push I needed to claim my girl. She's the reason we're here now.

"I'll move in with you."

My eyes spring open.

"I'll move in with you," Arwen repeats, a bright smile spreading across her face. "But I want something first, Granger."

"Anything," I growl. I'll give her the fucking world if she asks for it.

Her blue eyes darken as she reaches for the tie of her robe. The knot slips free, the front parting. Tantalizing flashes of her alabaster flesh peep out at me, sapping the moisture from my mouth. She takes a step backward in the apartment and then another.

I follow. Of course I do.

"You," she whispers. "I want you."

Epilogue One

Granger

Six Years Later

"My mommy used ta be a model," Rue announces to her grandpa at dinner, patting his cheek. "It's how my daddy falled in lub with her."

I nearly choke on my steak.

"Really?" Luna says, looking at Arwen with wide eyes. "When did you model?"

"She modeled with her boys, grammy."

This time, Carter chokes on his steak.

"What the fuck?" he growls at Arwen, making our twin boys giggle. They're only two. They think it's hysterical whenever anyone says a bad word. Frankly, I'm just glad they finally grew out of repeating them. Arwen was going to kill me and Carter both if they shouted fuck one more time.

"Voice," Arwen quickly says to our almost four-year-old. "I modeled with my voice, baby girl."

"Boys," Rue repeats, narrowing her eyes on Arwen. "That's what I said."

Luna laughs quietly, her expression soft. "She's just like you when you were her age," she says to Arwen, who smiles at her mom. "But what exactly is a voice model?"

Arwen's smile slips. Her gaze darts in my direction. We've always edited this part of our story out when telling everyone how we met. But I knew it was only a matter of time before someone found out once Arwen told Rue. Our daughter can't keep a secret to save her life.

Fuck it. We might as well confess. Luna won't give up until Arwen spills. She and my wife are exactly alike in that way. Secrets drive them crazy. They want to know everything about everything every moment of the day. It's fucking adorable.

"When we were replacin' the roof of her building, she went to work as a phone S-E-X operator," I say, spelling it out so the kids don't start asking questions they're far too young to be asking. "I made sure no one called her but me."

She quit the job right after we got together. I didn't ask her to do it, but I think she knew I wouldn't quit calling so long as she was working. I'm a possessive asshole. Sue me. I don't want anyone talking dirty to her, not for any reason. She's mine to take care of, mine to support. She came to work for me instead, running my office when she wasn't in class. We spent more time fucking on my desk than anything. It's exactly how she ended up pregnant with Rue.

"You..." Carter takes a deep breath, glaring at me and then at Arwen, and then at me again. "I knew you defiled my little girl, you B-A-S-T-A-R-D."

"Carter Grayson!" Luna growls at her husband.

"Daddy!" Arwen admonishes.

"It's true," he mutters, unrepentant.

I just shrug, not holding it against him. It is true, not that I'm telling him that. He's an incredible father, and he's wrapped around Arwen's little finger. He gives me shit at every available opportunity, but he welcomed me to the family a long time ago. He might not have chosen me for his little girl, but he wouldn't change anything either. He knows she belongs with me.

Truthfully, I think he appreciates that she picked someone like me and not a fucking pushover. She's insatiably curious and so damn beautiful and sweet. She needs someone like me keeping assholes away from her. I still take that job seriously. No one touches my wife and kids. No one comes close. They're mine to love, mine to protect. They are the best part of my life. I know I'm the best part of theirs too. They complete me.

"What's depiled?" Rue asks.

"It's what happens when two grown-ups love each other very much," Luna says, smiling at Rue.

"Oh," Rue says, and then she giggles. "Then my daddy depiles my mommy lots."

"Jesus Christ," I mutter as Arwen and Luna both devolve in a fit of giggles. Carter glares at me over the top of Rue's head. As if he has any room to talk. I caught him feeling up his wife in the hall not even ten minutes before dinner.

Frankly, I can't fucking wait to be the same way he and Luna are when we're their age. I know I'll still love his daughter the same way then that I do now. It might have taken the threat of losing her to some other motherfucker to get me moving, but I'm a quick study and, I don't make the same mistake twice. She's mine now and she will be until I take my dying breath. And then? Well, I hope phones are still around in whatever life comes next. Because I'll be finding her there too.

I'll always find her. I'll always love her.

If we're put on this earth for a purpose, she's mine.

Epilogue Two
Arwen

Ten Years Later

    "On your knees," Granger growls. "Ass in the air, cheek against the pillow, little one."

I scramble to obey, biting my lip to keep from sobbing his name. He's been toying with me for hours already, driving me right to the edge of orgasm and then backing off, only to start all over again. My entire body is overly sensitive. My brain is sluggish, and my movements jerky. Even the air against my overheated skin feels like too much.

I need him inside me now.

"Easy, baby doll," he croons, running a hand across my ass when I'm in position.

He steps up behind me, the heat of his body making me sob his name.

"You need to come, don't you?"

"Yes. Please, Granger," I plead, not above begging if that's what it takes. "Please let me come."

"Why should I, little one?" he growls, leaning down to attack the side of my throat with his lips. His hand slips between my legs, his thumb homing in on my clit with startling accuracy as he begins his wicked torment all over again. "You've been teasin' me all fucking week because you knew I couldn't do anything about it. You sent me all those sexy pictures. You touched my pussy on camera and made me watch you do it. You've been torturin' me."

"I'm sorry!" I sob, rocking back against his hand.

"No, you aren't."

He's right. I'm not sorry. I just spent a week in Sacramento for work, and I missed him horribly. I spent the whole time making sure he missed me just as much. I teased him mercilessly every day, knowing he couldn't do anything about it. I wanted to watch him unravel. I wanted to watch him crack. It's been ten years, and this man still drives me wild. But we don't have nearly as much time to play as we did ten years ago. With kids underfoot, finding time can be difficult.

Not today. When he picked me up from the airport, the kids were nowhere to be found. And my man was in beast mode. I've been paying for my teasing since we pulled into the driveway. I never want it to stop. And yet, if he doesn't let me come soon, there might not be enough of me left *to* orgasm when he finally lets me.

He rips his hand away as soon as I'm on the edge again.

"Granger!" I shout. "Please!"

His hand comes down on my ass in a hard smack.

I sob his name, pain bleeding to ecstasy as my hips rock forward.

He grabs me, dragging me right back into position. His palm runs across my cheek, soothing the sting. "Goddamn, baby doll," he breathes. "You look good in red."

"More," I beg.

"You aren't supposed to enjoy your punishment."

We both know he's lying. The only punishment he ever gives me is the kind we both enjoy. The kind I live and breathe for. After ten years, there's nothing we haven't done together. No fantasy we haven't indulged. No desire we haven't uncovered. But this is my favorite. Granger in control, taking what he wants, how he wants.

Phone sex with him ten years ago was incredible. But nothing competes with this man when I've pushed him past the breaking point. Nothing compares to my husband when he's driving me out of my mind. He knows me better than anyone. He knows my body better than I do.

He smacks my other cheek, making me cry out his name.

"You sound so sweet when you're sobbing my name, Arwen." He yanks me back toward him. "But I want to hear you scream it." He enters me in one deep thrust, impaling me on his hard cock.

I come instantly, screaming exactly like he wanted.

"Good girl," he croons, his voice guttural as he grips my hip tight to hold me in place. As the orgasm rips me apart with savage intensity, he drives into me, his hips crashing against mine to drive him deeper.

I writhe in ecstasy, tears slipping down my cheeks as he wrecks me in the best way possible. There's nothing I can do except take it. Take it. Take it. One orgasm bleeds into another, my nipples dragging across the bedding. His name leaves my lips in loud cracks of sound that only spur him on.

"Give me one more, baby doll," he demands. "I want to feel that tight cunt squeezing me while I'm claiming your womb."

"Granger," I whimper.

"It belongs to me, little one," he growls. "You're the reason I need to come. I'm breeding you again when I do it." He tilts my hips higher, changing the angle slightly. "Besides, we both know how much you love when I leave you dripping my cum."

I moan as my stomach clenches...just like it always does when he talks about breeding me. There's something ungodly sexy about this man coming inside me and wanting to get me pregnant at every available opportunity. He makes me want it just as badly.

" I'm putting another baby in you, Arwen." He slips his hand between my legs. "Christ. You've made a mess of this little thing for me." His fingers slip through my folds, his thumb circling my clit. "Now it's my turn. Fucking come, little one."

I try to ignore the command and drag this out for as long as possible, but my body is under his spell as much now as it's ever been. There is no holding it off. As soon as I feel his teeth close around the shell of my ear, my entire body seizes up.

I wail his name as I fall apart beneath him, collapsing into an orgasm powerful enough to leave me seeing stars. My lungs stop functioning. For one perfect moment, the entire world disappears. All that's left is his weight against my back, his teeth around my ear, and his hard length inside me, fucking me as if he never intends to stop.

My name echoes around the room, shouted from his lips in pure ecstasy as my body clamps down on his. He loses his rhythm and his mind at the same time. He fucks me wildly, pumping his hips and cursing as cum shoots up his shaft and then splashes inside me, hot and sticky. Perfect.

We tremble together. Moan together.

And then we collapse together.

Granger rolls to the side, dragging me into his arms. His heart pounds like a drum against my back, his arms shaking around me. He kisses the back of my neck again and again, pelting my skin with adoring kisses and panted breaths.

"Are you okay, baby doll?" he asks, checking in with me like he always does.

"Perfect," I promise.

"Yeah, you are." His lips touch the back of my neck, lingering. And then he groans and drags himself from the bed before lifting me into his arms. "Come on. Let's get you into the bath."

I hum my agreement, resting my head against my shoulder. This right here is my favorite part of our time together. The quiet moments afterward. It's been ten years, and he still treats me like a princess. Especially after he's rough with me. I love it so much.

I love him even more. I would never have imagined that going to work as a phone sex operator could have turned out like this, but I'm glad it did. My one and only client is the love of my life, and my life is magical because of him.

What more could a girl possibly want?

Author's Note

If you enjoyed Come Undone, please consider leaving a review!

Want more Love Bites? Check out Lola's story, Dripping Pearls! It is now available!

Dripping Pearls

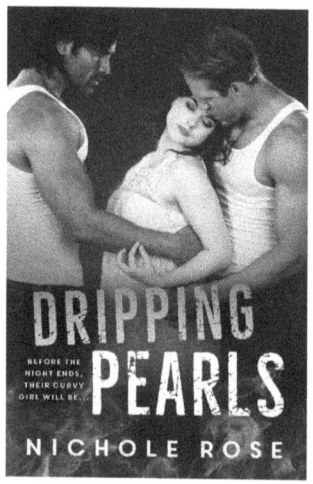

By the end of the night, their curvy girl will be dripping pearls.

Lola Knight

When I took a summer job working for my idols, I thought my life was complete.

And then I met them in person and fell in love.

They're opposites in every way, but like a moth to the flame, I'm drawn to both.

I crave their touches. Their kisses. Their love.

I don't think I stand a chance until a summer storm strands me with the men of my dreams and the rules go out the window.

As it turns out, they have a few desires of their own.

They say they're going to claim me, own me...ruin me.

Tonight, I'm going to let them.

But I don't want this to end when the storm does.

I want Liam and Braxton forever.

If you enjoy your curvy girl romance quick, dirty, and over-the-top, you'll love Dripping Pearls, a short MMF office romance. Dripping Pearls is a standalone addition to the Love Bites series. It is available here.

Nichole's Book Beauties

Want to connect with Nichole and other readers? We're building a girl gang! Join Nichole Rose's Book Beauties on Facebook for fun, games, and behind-the-scenes exclusives!

Instalove Book Club

The Instalove Book Club is now in session!

Get the inside scoop from your favorite instalove authors, meet new authors to love, and snag a free book and bonus content from featured authors every month. The Instalove Book Club newsletter goes out once per week!

Join the Club: http://instalovebookclub.com

Follow Nichole

Sign-up for Nichole's mailing list at http://authorni
cholerose.com/newsletter to stay up to date on all new
releases and for exclusive ARC giveaways from Nichole
Rose.

Want to connect with Nichole and other readers? Join
Nichole Rose's Book Beauties on Facebook!

f

facebook.com/AuthorNicholeRose/

instagram.com/AuthorNicholeRose

twitter.com/AuthNicholeRose

bookbub.com/authors/nichole-rose

tiktok.com/@authornicholerose

Also by Nichole Rose

Claimed Series
Possessing Liberty

Teaching Rowan

Claiming Caroline

Kissing Kennedy

Claimed: The Complete Series

Love on the Clock Series
Adore You

Hold You

Keep You

Protect You

Love on the Clock: The Complete Series

The Billionaires' Club
The Billionaire's Big Bold Weakness

The Billionaire's Big Bold Wish

The Billionaire's Big Bold Woman

The Billionaire's Big Bold Wonder

The Billionaires' Club: The Complete Series

Playing for Keeps
Cutie Pie

Ice Breaker

Ice Prince

Ice Giant

Cold as Ice

Ice Storm (coming soon)

Full-Length Titles

Crash into You

Fight for You (coming soon)

Kill for You (coming soon)

The Second Generation

A Blushing Bride for Christmas

Love Bites

Come Undone

Dripping Pearls

Echoes of Forever

His Christmas Miracle

Taken by the Hitman

Wicked Saint

The Ruined Trilogy
Physical Science

Wrecked

Wanton

Wicked

Destination Romance
Romancing the Cowboy

Beach House Beauty

Standalone Titles
A Touch of Summer

Black Velvet

His Secret Obsession

Dirty Boy

Naughty Little Elf

Tempted by December

Devil's Deceit

A Bride for the Beast (writing with Fern Fraser)

A Hero for Her

Pretty Little Mess

Dear Mr. Dad Bod

Easy on Me

Easy Ride

Easy Surrender

One Night with You

Falling Hard

Model Behavior

Learning Curve

Angel Kisses

Silver Spoon MC

The Surgeon

The Heir

The Lawyer

The Prodigy

The Bodyguard

Silver Spoon MC Collection: Nichole's Crew

Silver Spoon Falls

Xavier's Kitten

Callum's Hope

Snow's Prince

Aurora's Knight

<u>Silver Spoon Falcons</u>

Leia's Playmaker

Aspen's Defense (coming soon)

Gabbi's Goalie (coming soon)

<u>writing with Loni Ree as Loni Nichole</u>

Dillon's Heart

Razor's Flame

Ryker's Reward

Zane's Rebel

Oral Arguments

Grizz's Passion

Garrett's Obsession

About Nichole Rose

Nichole Rose writes filthy, feel-good romance for curvy readers. Her books feature headstrong, sassy women and the alpha males who consume them. From grumpy detectives to country boys with attitude to instalove and over-the-top declarations, nothing is off-limits.

Nichole is sure to have a steamy, sweet story just right for everyone. She fully believes the world is ugly enough without trying to fit falling in love into a one-size-fits-all box.

When not writing, Nichole enjoys fine wine, cute shoes, and everything supernatural. She is happily married to the love of her life and is a proud mama to the world's most ridiculous fur-babies. She and her husband live in Arkansas.

You can learn more about Nichole and her books at authornicholerose.com.

facebook.com/AuthorNicholeRose/

instagram.com/AuthorNicholeRose

twitter.com/AuthNicholeRose

bookbub.com/authors/nichole-rose

tiktok.com/@authornicholerose

Milton Keynes UK
Ingram Content Group UK Ltd.
UKHW022017020124
435341UK00014B/250